EXTREME SURVIVAL

SURVIVING DISASTERS

Nick Hunter

Chicago, Illinois

www.heinemannraintree.com
Visit our website to find out
more information about
Heinemann-Raintree books.

To order:

☎ Phone 888-454-2279
🖥 Visit www.heinemannraintree.com
to browse our catalog and order online.

© 2011 Raintree
an imprint of Capstone Global Library, LLC
Chicago, Illinois

Visit our website at
www.heinemannraintree.com

Edited by Adam Miller, Adrian Vigliano, and Andrew
Farrow
Designed by Steve Mead
Original illustrations © Capstone Global Library Ltd.
Illustrated by Jeff Edwards
Picture research by Tracy Cummins
Production by Camilla Crask
Originated by Capstone Global Library Ltd
Printed and bound in the United States of America,
North Mankato, MN

15 14 13 12 11
10 9 8 7 6 5 4 3 2 1

Library of Congress Cataloging-in-Publication Data

Hunter, Nick.
  Surviving disasters / Nick Hunter. — 1st ed.
    p. cm. — (Extreme survival)
  Includes bibliographical references and index.
  ISBN 978-1-4109-3971-5 (hc)
  ISBN 978-1-4109-3978-4 (pb)
  1. Disasters. 2. Survival skills. I. Title.
  HC79.D45.H86 2011
  613.6´9—dc22   2010028838

Acknowledgments
The author and publishers are grateful to the
following for permission to reproduce copyright
material: AP Photo pp. **4**, **36**, **28** (Andrew Brownbill),
18 (Diario del Sur), **27** (LM Otero); Corbis pp. **41**
(©Arko Datta), **40** (©BENOIT TESSIER/Reuters),
30 & 31 (©Bill Stormont), **5** (©Frans Lanting), **8**
(©Enny Nuraheni/Reuters), **11** (©Erik De Castro/
Reuters), **29** (©GENE BLEVINS/Reuters), **24** (©Jim
Edds), **34** (© Jorge Uzon), **19** (©Kim Kulish), **44**
(©Larry Downing/Reuters), **15** (©Leo La Valle/epa),
13 (©Steve Crisp/Reuters); Getty Images pp. **37**
(Eric Hoarau/TAAF/AFP), **6** (Jewel Samad/AFP), **39**
(Jose Jimenez/Primera Hora), **23** (Marko Georgiev),
16 (Per-Anders Pettersson/Liaison), **38** (Robert
Giroux), **7** (Roberto Schmidt/AFP), **32** (Rolls Press/
Popperfoto), **46** (Space Frontiers), **25** (Steven Pratt),
42 (Tyler Stableford), **22** (Vincent Laforet/AFP), **43**
(WALDIE/AF); istockphoto p. **45** (©Julia Nichols);
NASA p. **47**; Shutterstock pp. **49** (©Aleksey Fursov),
9 (©Christophe Testi); Visuals Unlimited, Inc. p. **21**
(Dr. Richard Roscoe).

Cover photograph of Hurricane Katrina reproduced
with the permission of Corbis/Jim Reed.

We would like to thank Ann Fullick for her invaluable
help in the preparation of this book.

Every effort has been made to contact copyright
holders of any material reproduced in this book. Any
omissions will be rectified in subsequent printings if
notice is given to the publisher.

Disclaimer

CONTENTS

Some words are printed in bold, **like this**. You can find out what they mean by looking in the glossary.

EXTREME SURVIVAL

It was Christmas Eve, 1971, high over the Amazon rain forest. A plane battled its way through a fierce storm. Juliane Koepcke, a 17-year-old German high school student, was flying with her mother from Lima, Peru, to Pucallpa, in the Amazon. Juliane was going to meet her father for Christmas—but the plane never arrived. It was struck by lightning and exploded midair. The passengers fell 3 kilometers (2 miles) into the forest.

Astonishingly, Juliane survived the plunge to the ground. She saw no other survivors, so she had to find help in the huge forest. Juliane found a stream. She remembered her father saying that following water downstream would lead to people. She waded along the stream, avoiding crocodiles and deadly fish called piranhas. Eventually, Juliane reached a hut, where local people tended to her injuries.

Fighting for survival

Juliane Koepcke was not an adventurer or an explorer. She was an ordinary girl caught up in an amazing fight for survival. This book will recount the true stories of other ordinary people who have survived natural disasters such as earthquakes and **tsunamis**. We will look at how people have overcome the world's most extreme weather. The book will also tell tales of courage and **endurance** in the face of human-made disasters, from air crashes to **terrorist** attacks. Each chapter will include tips on the best ways to survive in a variety of extreme circumstances, while also asking what we can learn from the experiences of those who survived.

Juliane Koepcke, after returning from her dramatic survival adventure in the rain forest. Juliane went on to work as a zoologist.

WHAT DOES IT TAKE

The true stories in this book show us that we could all find ourselves in a survival situation. What are the qualities, skills, and knowledge that would help a person pull through? A later chapter asks you to consider how you would react in some of these situations. Would you survive?

SURVIVING EARTHQUAKES

Just before 5 p.m. on January 12, 2010, the Caribbean country of Haiti was ripped apart by an earthquake. Haiti is a very poor country, and so many buildings there were not built to the high standards of safety expected in wealthier countries like the United States. After the earthquake, buildings were shattered across the country. Rescuers rushed to save those trapped inside, but more than 200,000 people died.

This is the royal palace in Port-au-Prince, Haiti, after it was destroyed by the earthquake of January 2010.

Fifteen days after the earthquake hit, teenager Darlene Etienne was pulled from the wreckage of her house. Neighbors had heard a voice inside and urged rescuers to investigate, even though the official search for survivors had been called off four days earlier. Darlene was extremely weak after her two-week ordeal. She survived because she was able to breathe where she lay, and rescuers believe that she was able to drink bathwater. She was lucky that she did not have any serious injuries that caused her to lose blood or get an infection.

Darlene Etienne was treated by French medical workers after her amazing escape from the rubble of her home.

TALES OF SURVIVAL

The loss of life in Haiti was tragic. But there were many individual tales of survival among the ruins. For example, 24-year-old Wismond Exantus survived for 11 days in the grocery store where he worked. He was able to survive under a desk, which protected him from the collapse of the building. He lived on some of the store's supply of soft drinks and cookies.

Predicting earthquakes

Earthquakes usually strike without warning. The ground begins to shake and, within seconds, buildings, roads, and bridges are destroyed.

Small underground **tremors** (vibrations) can happen anywhere. But larger earthquakes normally strike at particular areas of Earth's **crust** (outer layer). The land around the edge of the Pacific Ocean is known as the "Ring of Fire," because there are so many earthquakes and volcanic eruptions there. Many large cities throughout the world, from Tokyo to San Francisco, are built on areas where major quakes can happen.

Aftereffects

Many of those who die in earthquakes are killed by the immediate impact, such as the collapse of buildings. But more dangers linger after the initial earthquake. Mudslides and **tsunamis** (see pages 12 to 15) can be triggered by the quake. Immediately after the quake, broken pipes can cause gas leaks, explosions, and fires. It is also very common for **aftershocks** to follow the first impact for several days afterward. Aftershocks are smaller tremors that can destroy buildings already weakened by the main quake.

Dangers

People who manage to survive all these dangers still face disease and **dehydration** (lack of water). This is because clean water supplies may be disrupted, and earthquake damage can make it very difficult for supplies to reach people. **Contaminated** water can carry disease.

This mudslide in Sumatra, Indonesia was triggered by an earthquake in October 2009. The aftereffects of an earthquake can be just as dangerous as the quake itself.

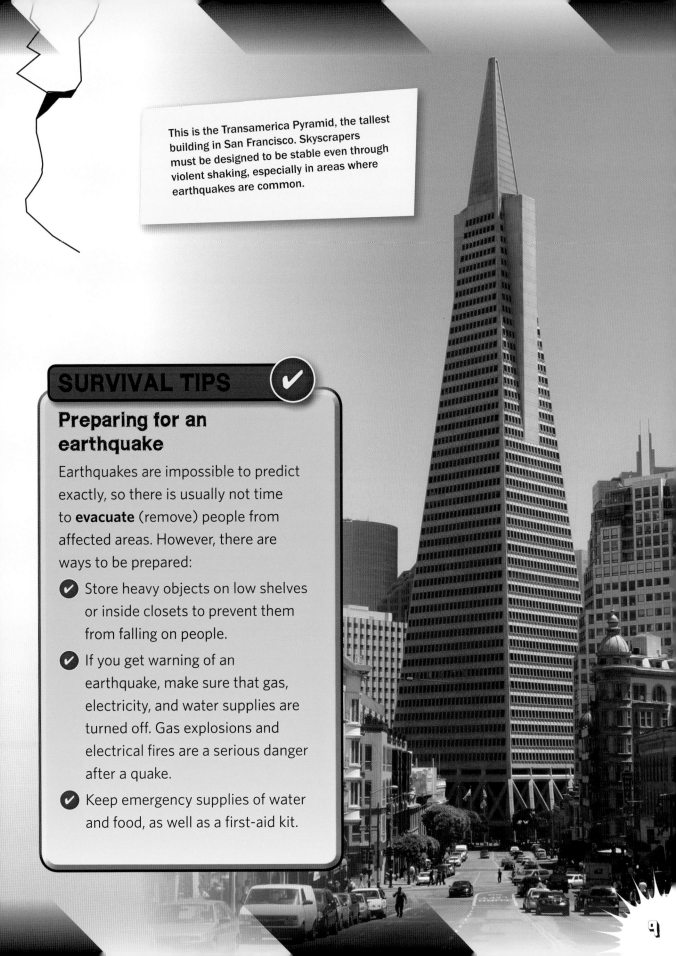

This is the Transamerica Pyramid, the tallest building in San Francisco. Skyscrapers must be designed to be stable even through violent shaking, especially in areas where earthquakes are common.

SURVIVAL TIPS ✔

Preparing for an earthquake

Earthquakes are impossible to predict exactly, so there is usually not time to **evacuate** (remove) people from affected areas. However, there are ways to be prepared:

- ✔ Store heavy objects on low shelves or inside closets to prevent them from falling on people.

- ✔ If you get warning of an earthquake, make sure that gas, electricity, and water supplies are turned off. Gas explosions and electrical fires are a serious danger after a quake.

- ✔ Keep emergency supplies of water and food, as well as a first-aid kit.

Amazing earthquake survivors

Despite all the incredible dangers, many people do survive earthquakes. Some people go through incredible hardship, though. The following are some amazing examples of earthquake survivors:

1985 Twenty-two newborn babies are discovered after 9 days in the ruins of a hospital in Mexico City.

1995 Park Seung Hyun is rescued from a collapsed supermarket in Seoul, South Korea, after 16 days.

2004 Shahr-Banu Mazandarani is rescued from her collapsed home 9 days after an earthquake in Iran. She was 97 years old.

2005 Naqsha Bibi is rescued from the kitchen of her collapsed house in Kashmir after 63 days. She survived on rotting food and water trickling into the kitchen.

2010 Evans Muncie is rescued from a collapsed market in Haiti after 28 days.

SURVIVAL SCIENCE

Surviving under rubble

As we have seen, people can survive under collapsed buildings for many days. But what does the body need to keep going, and how long can people survive under such conditions?

Air: The gas **oxygen** is essential for life. If people are totally buried with no access to air, they will not be able to survive.

Water: The human body can only survive for three to six days without water. On average we require about 2.4 liters (around five pints) of water per day to survive.

Food: Although food is essential for life, a healthy human body can survive for about eight weeks without it.

Injuries: It is important that survivors have not been badly injured in the earthquake. Loss of blood will probably be fatal. Untreated wounds may also become badly infected.

Emotions: Survivors need to try to remain calm. Their bodies will use less energy and water if they reduce stress and do not try to move.

Surviving an earthquake

If you ever experience an earthquake, keep these tips in mind:

- ✔ If you are outside when an earthquake strikes, stay away from tall buildings and lie on the ground. The best place to be is in an open space.

- ✔ If you are in a car, stop the car, but stay inside it for protection.

- ✔ If you are inside, move away from windows. If possible, take shelter under a strong table or desk. Never go in an elevator during or after an earthquake.

- ✔ If you are in a multilevel building, lower floors are safer than higher ones. Survivors may become trapped under **debris** (wreckage), but at least they will not have so far to fall themselves. However, you should avoid trying to move to a lower floor during an earthquake.

- ✔ Do not light matches or attempt to use electrical appliances. Sparks could cause explosions.

Students in the Philippines take cover under their desks during an earthquake drill.

SURVIVING RAGING WATERS

*December 26, 2004, seemed like just another day on the coasts around the Indian Ocean. People went about their daily lives from Indonesia to Sri Lanka. Vacationers relaxed on the beaches of Thailand. But many hundreds of thousands of lives were about to change. Beneath the Indian Ocean, off the coast of Indonesia, a massive earthquake launched a series of huge waves, or **tsunamis**. These waves crashed ashore across the region and claimed more than 200,000 lives.*

Surviving in Sri Lanka

As the tsunami crossed the Indian Ocean, traveling at hundreds of miles per hour, the *Queen of the Sea* train was carrying about 1,500 passengers along the coast of Sri Lanka, toward the city of Galle. Suddenly, the train was engulfed by the tsunami waters.

The train flipped over four times and filled with water. Daya Wijaya Gunawardana was traveling with his family to visit relatives. He was able to escape the train through a window once it stopped moving, although the train car he was in had filled with water. But more than 800 other people died there, in what would become the world's worst train disaster. Survivors headed to high ground, fearing more waves.

Surviving in Indonesia

In Indonesia, more than 130,000 people were killed by the tsunami. Despite the huge loss of life, there are many amazing stories of survivors there as well.

Eight days after the tsunami, a sailor on a container ship spotted a man in the sea, clinging to branches about 160 kilometers (100 miles) off the coast of Sumatra, Indonesia. Rizal Shahputra had been cleaning a building on the tip of the island when the tsunami hit. He was swept out to sea, along with many other people. He survived by drinking rainwater and eating coconuts, which had also been taken out to sea by the giant waves. He broke the coconut shells using a doorknob from a door he found drifting in the water.

The city of Banda Aceh in Indonesia was devastated by the tsunami of December 2004. These survivors returned to discover that their houses had been destroyed.

The blue circle in the center of the map shows where the underwater earthquake struck on December 26, 2004. The circles moving out from there show where the tsunami waves traveled from the point of the earthquake.

No warning

Tsunamis like the one in 2004, are fortunately very rare. The 2004 earthquake was the third-most-powerful quake ever recorded. It caused a huge shift in the seabed that unleashed the massive walls of water.

One of the reasons why so many lives were lost in 2004 is that there was very little warning. People did not know they should move to high ground. This lack of warning was because tsunamis are very hard to detect, and can move incredibly fast. Although they can travel hundreds of miles across the ocean, the underwater earthquake that started them may not be felt on land at all.

The trough, or low point, of the wave usually arrives first. This acts like a vacuum, sucking water away from the coast. This happened in Thailand in 2004. The ocean water pulled back, leaving huge spaces of seabeds exposed. Many people walked out into those areas to see what was happening and were not able to escape in time when giant waves came racing in.

SURVIVAL TIPS

Surviving a tsunami

If there is a warning of a tsunami, or if **tremors** are felt near the coast, people should move toward higher ground far away from the coast. The force of a tsunami can carry water far inland. Much of its destructive power comes from the **debris** that it carries, such as furniture, cars, and rocks. So, get as far away from the water as possible.

SURVIVAL SCIENCE

Surviving in the water

The sheer force of the swirling water is one thing that makes a tsunami so destructive. Many of those who survived the 2004 tsunami, such as those on the Sri Lankan train, were underwater for a long time. There is no air to breathe underwater. Drowning happens when the victim breathes water rather than air into the lungs. Being in water for long periods can also lead to **hypothermia** (a drop in the core body temperature).

Future warnings

One result of the disaster was that a tsunami warning system was put in place around the Indian Ocean. It is hoped that this will ensure that people will be better warned about tsunamis in the future.

If an earthquake is felt on land near the coast, it can also cause a tsunami. This happened in Chile in 2010.

Floods

Floods come in many forms. As we have seen, some are caused by tsunamis—but these are rare. Most floods are triggered by heavy rainfall, which can cause the water level in rivers to rise above raised areas of land, or banks, that run alongside them.

In some areas, such as along the Mississippi River, special raised banks called **levees** are built along rivers. These are used to help prevent regular flooding. But when the water rises above the levees, flooding can be **catastrophic**. Sometimes floods can also be caused by human-made structures, such as dams, bursting.

Floods usually affect river valleys and low-lying ground. If heavy rain falls after a long dry spell, flash floods can result. These sudden floods can be very destructive, particularly in steep-sided valley areas.

In 2000, the country of Mozambique in Africa was hit by devastating floods. People had to be rescued from the roofs of their homes. Several hundred people died but many more were affected by the loss of crops and cattle that they relied on for food.

BOSCASTLE

In 2004 the English fishing village of Boscastle was hit by a flash flood after heavy rain cascaded off the nearby hills and traveled through the steep-sided valley where the village lies. The village's bridge was destroyed. Many people were pulled to safety by helicopters. No one was killed, and things could have been much worse if people had not stayed in their homes and waited for rescue.

After the flood

Floodwaters normally carry wastewater and often animal and human remains. One of the biggest risks from floods is **contaminated** water and the spread of diseases such as cholera and typhoid. Both of these diseases are caused by **microorganisms** (tiny living things) in dirty water. They affect the intestines and can be deadly if they are not treated quickly.

In countries where people rely on crops and animals for their food, flooding can destroy their main food source. This makes surviving after the flood even more difficult.

SURVIVAL TIPS

Surviving a flood

The following are some tips to keep in mind if you ever encounter a flood:

- ✔ If you are warned of a flood, or suspect one is coming, head for high ground.
- ✔ If you are inside a flooded building, stay there. You will be safer on the upper floor of a building than walking or driving through floodwaters, which could be hiding all kinds of debris and other dangers such as exposed electrical cables.
- ✔ Floodwaters can cause lots of damage to buildings, so you should do whatever you can to seal doors and windows against flooding.
- ✔ You should try to gather warm clothing, emergency food and water supplies, and something to attract the attention of rescuers.
- ✔ Do not eat or drink anything that has been in contact with the floodwater.

ESCAPING VOLCANIC ERUPTIONS

*Like earthquakes, it is difficult to predict when volcanoes will erupt. **Volcanologists** risk their lives trying to understand volcanoes. They climb active volcanoes to carry out tests. On January 14, 1993, Stanley Williams and a team of volcanologists climbed to the top of Mount Galeras, in Colombia. They were there to find out more about how eruptions happen. But no one knew the volcano was about to erupt.*

The eruption of Mount Galeras in 1993 was a very minor one, but it was still enough to demonstrate the volcano's deadly power.

Rockfalls inside the volcano alerted the team that something was happening, so they began to leave. At 1:41 p.m., the volcano erupted with a roar, throwing tons of rocks and ash into the air. As the team ran down the volcano, Stanley was hit by a rock about the size of an orange, which crushed the side of his skull. He collapsed as white-hot rocks flew around him like bullets, breaking both his legs. Using his backpack to protect his head, he collapsed behind a boulder. The backpack and his clothes were now on fire.

Daring rescue

Stanley and his team had to hope that they would be rescued. Two of their colleagues bravely searched for survivors, and Stanley and three others were rescued. But several volcanologists were killed in the eruption. The volcano showed just how deadly it could be.

Dr. Stanley Williams did not let his brush with death on Mount Galeras stop him from continuing to climb volcanoes to discover why they erupt. Like all volcanologists, he hopes that by risking his life he will save other lives in the future.

PROTECTION FROM ASH AND ROCKS

Very few of those who ventured onto Mount Galeras in 1993 were wearing helmets and protective clothing. Helmets and fireproof clothing may not have saved lives in such a situation, but they may have prevented some of the head injuries and burns that the victims suffered.

Volcanic eruptions

Volcanic eruptions are an awesome demonstration of nature's power. There are many different types of eruption, but the heat and power generated by volcanoes means they are all very dangerous.

Major eruptions are a huge release of pressure beneath Earth's **crust**. Huge, white-hot boulders can be thrown hundreds of feet into the air, in addition to many smaller rock fragments.

Flows of **lava** from the sides of a volcano move at fairly slow rates. But with temperatures of up to 1,200˚C (2,200˚F), lava will destroy anything it touches.

Glowing cloud

More dangerous than anything else is the **pyroclastic flow**. This is a burning cloud of gas and dust—at around 700˚C (1,292˚F)—that moves down the slopes of the volcano at high speed. It burns anything in its path, leaving only ashes behind.

When Mount Pelee, on the Caribbean island of Martinique, erupted in 1902, one of these clouds killed 27,000 people in the city of St. Pierre. Some people burned to death in seconds, but others suffered hours with scorched throats and lungs.

SURVIVAL TIPS

Surviving a volcanic eruption

Most people will never be near a volcanic eruption. However, keep the following tips in mind if you ever find yourself in this situation:

- ✔ If a volcano erupts, you should **evacuate** the area immediately.
- ✔ If a pyroclastic flow is coming toward you, your best chance of survival is to completely submerge yourself in water.
- ✔ Volcanic ash will irritate the skin on contact, so you should try to cover yourself as much as possible. You should also try to cover your mouth and nose to prevent breathing in the dust. When combined with water in rainfall, the sulfur in volcanic ash creates sulfuric acid, which will burn skin on contact.

LIVING NEAR A VOLCANO

As Earth's population continues growing, more people live close to volcanoes than ever before. Mount Vesuvius, in Italy, erupted in 79 CE, burying the towns of Pompeii and Herculaneum. A few thousand people died in the eruption. If a similar eruption happened today without warning, it has been estimated that more than 100,000 people could die.

A deadly pyroclastic flow forms at this eruption of the Soufrière Hills volcano on the Caribbean island of Montserrat.

ENDURING EXTREME WEATHER

*The message was clear. Everyone who could leave the Gulf Coast area, spanning from central Florida to Texas, should **evacuate**. **Hurricane** Katrina, one of the strongest hurricanes ever recorded, was heading that way. On August 29, 2005, Katrina's strong winds and rain raged through the gulf.*

Hurricane Katrina hit the city of New Orleans, Louisiana, hardest of all. Many of the city's people had listened to the pleas to evacuate and had left. Others stayed because they had made it through hurricanes before, or because they were unable to leave their homes. Thousands took shelter in the Louisiana Superdome sports stadium.

When the Hurricane Katrina hit, water poured into low-lying parts of New Orleans.

The hurricane battered the city with furious power. Part of the roof of the Superdome was ripped off. Much of New Orleans is below sea level and is protected by **levees**. But the surging waters created by the hurricane broke these flood defenses. Suddenly, four-fifths of the city was flooded. The race was on to rescue the survivors.

Surviving the floods

Many people stayed in their homes. They had food and water supplies and hoped they could wait until the storm was over. The floods came so quickly that they had to be rescued, often from their roofs. Some painted messages on their roofs asking for help. Not all of them survived.

Food was also scarce. There were reports of gangs roaming the city, looting stores and anywhere else they could find food. Many tried to make their way to the Superdome in search of food, but the situation there was little better. Those who had taken shelter in the stadium were evacuated out of the city.

Boats and helicopters were the only ways to rescue people as lower storys of buildings were completely underwater.

PREPARING FOR DISASTER

Many people believe that the impact of Hurricane Katrina was made much worse by poor preparation. The levees that had been built to protect the city were built on soft ground and could not withstand the surging waters. There was also criticism that the Federal Emergency Management Agency (FEMA) was slow to react to the disaster and rescue those people who stayed.

Falling trees and flying materials can damage buildings and injure people during a hurricane.

Hurricane dangers

Hurricanes normally form in **tropical** areas. In Asia and the western Pacific, they are called typhoons or cyclones. Winds in a hurricane are usually over 119 kilometers per hour (74 miles per hour). These high winds are powerful enough to damage or destroy buildings and uproot trees.

Hurricanes also bring heavy rain. In coastal areas, the **storm surge** can be the most destructive part of a hurricane, as was the case with Katrina. A storm surge is a rise in sea level caused by a storm, which can lead to sudden and **catastrophic** flooding.

Predicting hurricanes

The tools of modern weather forecasting allow us to predict hurricanes. We can now use satellite technology to see when the swirling cloud pattern of a hurricane develops. Advance warning of hurricanes can be broadcast by radio. But even though hurricanes can be forecast, the path they take is not always predictable.

Surviving a hurricane

Hurricanes are huge forces of nature. If you get enough warning and you can move out of the path of a hurricane, that is the best thing to do. It is particularly important to move away from coastal or low-lying areas that may be affected by a storm surge. Here are some tips to keep in mind if you cannot get out of the path of the hurricane:

- ✔ Listen to regular radio or television reports on the path of the hurricane.
- ✔ Avoid being outside in a hurricane. The hurricane will pick up **debris**, including large items, parts of trees, and broken glass. But if you cannot avoid being outside, take shelter behind a solid structure or a large boulder. If you lie on the ground, you will be less of a target for flying objects.
- ✔ The best place to take shelter is in the middle of your house, away from doors and windows, ideally in a basement. Hurricane winds can tear off roofs.
- ✔ Board up all windows to prevent them from being broken by strong winds and flying debris.

STORM AT SEA

In 1979, 303 yachts set out on the Fastnet Race along the south coast of England. Their goal was to reach the Fastnet Rock, off the coast of Ireland. Strong winds were predicted, but nothing like the hurricane-force winds that hit the yachts. Fifteen people died, and many had to be rescued as boats were rolled completely over by the raging seas. In future races, all boats had to carry radios, to ensure that they would be warned of extreme weather.

Deadly twisters

The most powerful storms of all are **tornadoes**. These twisting funnels of wind affect a much smaller area than a hurricane. However, with wind speeds above 483 kilometers per hour (300 miles per hour), a tornado can rip a building from its foundation.

In February 2009, deadly tornadoes tore through Carter County, Oklahoma. Nine people were killed and hundreds were left homeless. One woman was almost sucked out through the roof of a house while she took shelter in a closet. Seven people taking shelter with her managed to hold onto her.

Tornadoes can happen anywhere, but many of the most dangerous tornadoes happen in the United States. And one-third of all U.S. tornadoes affect three states: Texas, Oklahoma, and Kansas. This region is known as "tornado alley." Warm air from the Gulf of Mexico meets cold air from Canada, which creates perfect conditions for the destructive twisters.

"The tornado crossed the road in front of us and hit a house. . . . In seconds, homes disappeared from their foundations." —Tim Marshall, storm chaser, Argonia, Kansas, 1991

SURVIVAL TIPS

Surviving a tornado

Here are some tips if you know a tornado has been spotted near you:

- ✔ If a warning is given for your area, you should find a very solid structure in which to take shelter. Do not take shelter in any lightweight structure, such as a trailer home or car. These could be picked up by the tornado.
- ✔ Once inside a structure, stay as far away from doors and windows as possible.
- ✔ Close the doors and windows on the side of the house facing the path of the tornado and open them on the other side. This may prevent the house from being sucked up by the twister.
- ✔ If you cannot find shelter and are in the open, run at a right angle away from the direction the tornado appears to be heading.

AVOIDING LIGHTNING STRIKES

It is estimated that lighting strikes kill almost as many people every year as tornadoes. If you are caught outside during a lightning storm, avoid being exposed on top of a hill. Never stand under an isolated tree or a boulder. If there is nowhere to take shelter, sit or lie on something dry and raised from the ground that will not conduct electricity. Do not touch the ground directly and do not hold any metal objects.

This house was ripped apart by a tornado in Lone Grove, Oklahoma in 2009.

FIGHTING FIRES

In dry areas, any spark can start a forest fire. Sometimes people create these sparks intentionally, but fires also begin naturally. Once forest fires catch hold, they spread very quickly and can stretch across many miles.

Victoria, Australia

In February 2009, the land in Victoria, Australia, was bone dry after a long period with no rain. Record temperatures and strong winds were predicted for Saturday, February 7, and so the government warned that there was a strong risk of forest fires. They were not wrong. The fires that raged across Victoria claimed 173 lives and destroyed whole towns.

The speed at which the flames spread was one reason why so many people died in the Victoria fires. Strong winds carry glowing fragments called embers away from the fire, and the embers then start new fires. Rescuers said that

February 7 became known as "Black Saturday" in Australia.

Forest fires have recently been a big problem in California.

many people waited before leaving their homes, and then it was too late to escape. Survivors described fleeing the fires in almost total darkness, apart from the glow of flames. As they drove through the burning bush (forest), their cars became incredibly hot.

Many people stayed to save their homes. One survivor, Steven Van Rooy, told a reporter how he and friends used hoses to delay the progress of the fire. When the heat became too much for them, they took shelter in a concrete bunker until the fire passed.

SURVIVAL TIPS

Surviving a forest fire

The first sign of a forest fire will usually be the smell of smoke. Here are some tips to keep in mind if you ever face a forest fire:

- ✔ In order to escape, you need to be aware of which way the wind is blowing. You should travel into the wind if it is blowing toward the fire. If the wind is blowing the fire toward you, find a firebreak such as a road or a river.
- ✔ Do not go toward high ground, because fire travels more quickly uphill.
- ✔ Some people have escaped fires by burying themselves in the earth until the fire has passed. This is very risky and should only be used as a last resort.

Fires in buildings

Forest fires can cover a wide area, but building fires can be just as dangerous.

Fire fighters are able to withstand fires because of equipment such as heavy, flame-resistant clothing, breathing masks, and oxygen tanks.

SURVIVAL SCIENCE

Fire and the body

When people are stuck near fires, breathing in smoke is just as dangerous as the flames. Breathing can be difficult, as the fire will take up much of the surrounding **oxygen**.

Contact with extreme heat or fire will cause the skin to burn. When the skin burns, blood **plasma** is lost. Plasma is the fluid part of the blood, and it is essential for blood to circulate properly. If a large area of skin is burned, the loss of plasma affects the whole body. Major burns can be deadly.

SURVIVAL TIPS

Surviving building fires

If you are ever in a building fire, keep these tips in mind:

✔ The first step if a fire is discovered is to try to smother it with a blanket or any piece of heavy fabric. You should not put water on an electrical fire unless the power is off.

✔ If the fire is already too fierce to put out, the building should be **evacuated**. As you exit, before entering any room, check that it is not on fire. Look for smoke around the edge of doors. Test the door handle to see if it is warm.

✔ If you have to escape through an upstairs window, make sure that there is soft material below to break your fall. Tie sheets and blankets together to make an improvised rope. This may not reach the ground, but it will reduce the distance of the fall.

✔ Sometimes the only way to escape is through the fire. If this happens, cover your head and body with a wet blanket.

✔ If your clothes catch fire during the escape, the best way to smother the flames is to stop, drop, and roll on the ground. Fire needs oxygen to burn, and this rolling procedure will prevent the air from getting to it.

✔ It is important to keep low to the ground in a fire to avoid inhaling smoke. Try to move around by crawling as there is often a layer of relatively clear air below the smoke.

CRASH COURSE IN SURVIVAL

On October 13, 1972, the Uruguayan rugby team was flying to play a game in Santiago, Chile. To reach Chile, the plane had to cross over the snow-capped Andes mountain range. The plane crashed in the heart of the Andes. Some of the 45 passengers died in the crash or shortly thereafter.

The survivors learned on a small radio that the search for them had been called off. This was many years before cell phones were available, so the survivors had no way to contact rescuers. They knew they had to survive on their own.

Surviving in the Andes

The survivors were not well prepared. They had no medical supplies to care for the injured. They also had to deal with the extreme cold without

After an incredibly long struggle, the survivors of the Andes crash desperately signal to their rescuers.

cold-weather clothing. Although they could melt snow to get fresh water, they had very little food. As days turned into weeks, they realized that their supplies would not last. They made the difficult decision to survive by eating the bodies of their dead co-passengers.

On December 12, two of the survivors set out across the mountains. After walking for 10 days, they found help. The last of the 16 survivors were rescued on December 23, after surviving for 72 days. Some were taken to the hospital, but all made a quick recovery and were able to tell their amazing story.

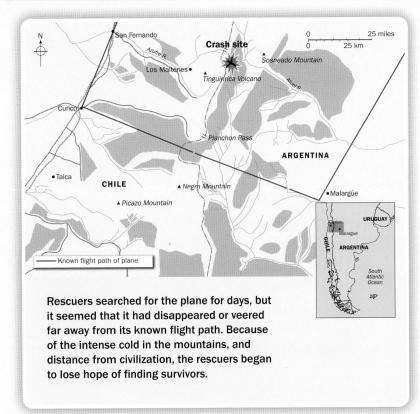

Rescuers searched for the plane for days, but it seemed that it had disappeared or veered far away from its known flight path. Because of the intense cold in the mountains, and distance from civilization, the rescuers began to lose hope of finding survivors.

SOLE SURVIVOR

There are many true stories of miraculous plane crash survivors:

In 1972 Vesna Vulovic, a flight attendant, fell 10,000 meters (33,000 feet) in the tail section of her plane. She landed in snow and suffered two broken legs, three broken vertebrae, a broken pelvis, and a fractured skull, but she survived. She was the only survivor of the crash.

When a Sudan Airways flight crashed shortly after takeoff in 2003, three-year-old Mohammed el-Fateh was the only survivor. He was reportedly found lying in a bush.

In 2009, 12-year-old Bahia Bakari was the only survivor of a Yemeni Airlines plane that crashed in the Indian Ocean. She survived by clinging to wreckage of the plane.

Surviving a plane crash

Surviving a plane crash is more likely than you might think. Of the about 53,000 people involved in plane crashes between 1983 and 2000, around 51,000 survived.

At Toronto's Pearson International Airport in August 2005, 309 passengers and crew members survived with only minor injuries when their plane burst into flames on landing. Highly trained crew members were able to **evacuate** the plane in two minutes, before passengers were overcome by smoke from the fire.

SAFEST SEATS

The safest seats on a plane depend on how the crash happens. Most experts think there is a greater chance of survival if a person is seated near the back of the plane. In a crash landing, the tail section will often become detached from the rest of the plane.

There are advantages to seats near the wings. There are usually exits over the wings, and this section is also more reinforced with steel. However, these seats are also close to the engines and fuel tanks, which are more likely to cause explosions and fires.

Many survivors of this crash and fire in Toronto praised the crew for organizing the evacuation so quickly.

SURVIVAL TIPS

Surviving a plane crash

Plane crashes are incredibly rare, but keep the following in mind if you are faced with one:

- ✔ Whenever you travel by plane, the flight attendants will show you where the nearest exit is, where to find a flotation device or life jacket, and other things you need to know in an emergency. Listen carefully to what they say.

- ✔ One of the things you might learn in the safety demonstration is how to get into a brace position. Bracing yourself against the seat in front of you will protect you from the forces generated when a plane comes to a sudden stop.

- ✔ Smoke and fumes can very quickly fill the cabin, and a plane is loaded with fuel that can cause an explosion. Therefore, make sure you know where your nearest exits are before the plane takes off. Count how many rows of seats there are between you and the exit. If a plane fills with smoke, you may need to rely on this number to find the exit.

SURVIVAL SCIENCE

Breathing in the sky

Airplanes usually fly at a height of about 11 kilometers (7 miles). At this height, the air is incredibly cold and contains very little **oxygen**. Aircraft cabins are pressurized to make them comfortable for passengers. Loss of this pressure for any reason would mean that passengers would be unable to breathe. If this happens in flight, oxygen masks will drop from the ceiling.

Abandon ship!

Most of Earth's surface is covered by water. History is full of stories of people who have survived against the odds at sea. Surviving alone on a vast ocean is a true battle against the elements.

In 1942 Poon Lim had to face such a battle. His ship was sunk by a German torpedo in the south Atlantic Ocean, on its way from Cape Town, South Africa, to South America. After jumping from the ship just before it sunk, Poon Lim was able to find a wooden life raft that carried some food and water. A canopy protected him from the burning sun.

Early in his ordeal, Poon Lim was hopeful that he would be rescued. A plane spotted him and dropped a marker **buoy**, but a storm separated him from the buoy and prevented his rescue. Realizing that his food and water would only last a short time, Poon Lim prepared to survive for as long as it took. He used material from his life jacket to collect rainwater and used a fishhook made from part of his flashlight to catch fish. He also caught a gull, using the fish as bait. With no way of cooking, Poon Lim ate his food raw.

Signs of land

After more than 130 days at sea, Poon Lim noticed that the sea was a different color and there were many more birds overhead. He must be nearing land. Shortly afterward, he was rescued by fishermen. He was close to the mouth of the Amazon River in South America. After 133 days in his life raft, he had survived.

The survival techniques that Poon Lim used during his 133 days at sea were later added to navy survival manuals.

Surviving at sea

The following tips can be used to help you survive in the unlikely event you are stranded at sea:

- ✔ In a cold climate, it is most essential to keep as warm and dry as possible. If your body loses too much heat, **hypothermia** can set in.

- ✔ To prevent sunburn and windburn, try to make sure your skin is covered at all temperatures.

- ✔ You should use every possible container to gather rainwater. Salt water will dry out the skin and cause boils over long periods. You also cannot drink salt water, as your body would need even more fresh water to process the salt.

- ✔ Readily available foods like fish and seaweed are high in protein, so they will also require extra water to digest them effectively.

Sixteen-year-old Abby Sunderland was months into her solo attempt to sail around the world, when her boat was badly damaged by high winds. Thanks to the advanced technology of distress beacons, rescuers were able to find her quickly even though she was stranded in a remote part of the Indian Ocean.

SURVIVING THE TWIN TOWERS

Sometimes the forces of nature or mechanical failure are not responsible for disasters. Instead, people sometimes deliberately cause disasters. This was the case with the terrifying destruction of the Twin Towers of the World Trade Center on September 11, 2001.

That morning, an airplane hit the North Tower of the World Trade Center at 8:46 a.m., crashing between the 92nd and 98th floors of the 110-story tower. At 9:02 a.m., another airplane hit the South Tower, crashing between its 78th and 85th floors. **Terrorists** had **hijacked** (overtaken) four passenger airplanes and flown two of them into the Twin Towers.

The Twin Towers were badly damaged when the planes hit them. But it was the intense heat from jet-fuel fires that eventually caused them both to collapse.

The collapse of the Twin Towers unleased a massive dust cloud throughout much of lower Manhattan. People tried to escape the cloud, due to concerns over breathing the dust.

Due to the structural damage and the heat caused by the explosions, both towers collapsed within two hours of the first attack. Most of the people in the floors below the impact had been able to **evacuate** before the collapses. For those in the highest floors, though, there was no way out. Over 2,700 people died as a result of the attacks. Many of them were rescue workers going in to save people.

Stanley Praimnath was on the phone in his 81st-floor office in the South Tower when he saw the plane coming toward the building. He dived under his desk as the plane crashed. Amid the tangle of wires and collapsed walls in his office, the plane's wing blocked the doorway. Stanley managed to crawl the length of the floor. His shouts attracted the attention of Brian Clark, who was trying to find a way out of the building. Together, they managed to escape the building before it collapsed.

LEARNING LESSONS

The attacks of September 11 had a huge impact on people in the United States, and around the world. After the attacks, more attention was paid to evacuation plans for similar buildings. In the World Trade Center, each tower only had three stairwells for people to evacuate, and these were close together in the core of the building. Had they been in different parts of the building, there may have been more chance of escape for those above the areas where the planes hit.

Last men out

Sergeant John McLoughlin of the New York Port Authority had worked at the World Trade Center for many years. He was in an underground area below the towers with four colleagues when the South Tower collapsed. Before they could free themselves, the North Tower also collapsed.

John McLoughlin and Will Jimeno were the only two members of their team still alive, but they were buried deep in rubble. As darkness fell on September 11, two marines heard the men's cries for help. It took many hours to free them. Rescue workers dug into the rubble, fearing that it might collapse further at any time. Will was freed at 11 p.m. John was the last survivor to be dug out of the World Trade Center ruins, at 7 a.m. on September 12. He underwent months of surgery and treatment to walk again.

"Initially, I thought I had died. I lost all sense. I had no sight. I had no smell. I had no hearing. Everything was just silent." —Sergeant John McLoughlin talks about the moment after the collapse of the South Tower of the World Trade Center

AIRPORT SECURITY

Since terrorists hijacked planes and flew them into the World Trade Center, there have been lots of improvements in airport security. In 2009 a new threat emerged when a passenger attempted to explode a bomb in his pants on a plane traveling to Detroit, Michigan. Partly in response to this, full-body scanners (see photo) have now been introduced at many airports.

The Taj Mahal hotel in Mumbai. The hotel was attacked partly because it was popular with foreign visitors and tourists.

Attack on Mumbai

Unfortunately, the September 11 attacks were not the only terrorist attacks of recent years. In November 2008, gunmen attacked a number of targets in Mumbai, India, including the railroad station, two hotels, and cafés visited by foreign tourists. Survivors of the attacks in the 600-room Taj Mahal Hotel hid in their rooms and tried to barricade doors to escape the attackers.

SURVIVAL TIPS

Surviving a terrorist attack

As with many of the disasters covered in this book, the chances of getting caught in a terrorist incident are very small. But there are some precautions you can take to lessen the risk even further:

✔ When planning to travel to somewhere unfamiliar, it is always a good idea to check government travel advice. Sometimes particular places will be listed as not safe for tourists.

✔ Of course, terrorism can happen anywhere. But attacks since 2001 have focused on high-profile targets in major cities. In public places, stay alert to what is going on around you. If police are evacuating an area, follow their instructions quickly and calmly.

WHEN DISASTER STRIKES

Some disasters affect people because of the jobs they do. Some people go to work every day knowing that they could find themselves in a survival situation. Emergency services such as the police and firefighters deal with disasters of one kind or another on a daily basis.

Mining is a job that can be very dangerous when things go wrong. Miners work in cramped and dirty conditions deep underground. Gases can be released that cause explosions. In April 2010, 29 miners died in an explosion in Montcoal, West Virginia. It was the worst U.S. mining disaster in many years.

Surviving underground

In 2006, two miners in Tasmania, Australia, were trapped underground when a small earth **tremor** caused a rockfall in the Beaconsfield gold mine. One of their fellow miners was killed.

It took five days for rescuers to discover that two men were still alive and trapped in the mine. Brant Webb and Todd Russell were surviving by drinking water that seeped through the rock.

Working deep underground can never be entirely risk-free, although mining today is much safer than it was in the past.

Their only food was a cereal bar, which they shared until six days into their ordeal. At that point, they were given food through a hole that was drilled. There was still a lot of work to do to get the miners out, though, as rescuers drilled through rock "five times as hard as concrete." The two men were trapped underground for two full weeks.

Todd Russell (left) and Brant Webb (center) greet the outside world excitedly after being rescued from their underground ordeal.

TRAFFIC ACCIDENTS

Some disasters, such as traffic accidents, may not be big news in the same way an earthquake or a plane crash might be. But the people involved need to think and act quickly to survive. The World Health Organization estimates that over 1.2 million people die in road accidents every year. Road accidents kill far more people than any of the other disasters covered in this book.

Radiation

In 1985 an accident at the Chernobyl nuclear plant in Ukraine sent a cloud of **radiation** across Europe. Radiation is made up of tiny particles that can harm people's health, causing cancer and a variety of other serious health problems. Radiation is invisible, so it is difficult to detect without specialized equipment. When it is released into an area, local food and water supplies can become **contaminated**.

Invisible dangers

There are some **hazardous** (dangerous) materials and survival situations that are not visible to the naked eye. Hazardous chemicals are produced in many factories. But if they escape into the air, they can be extremely dangerous. Industrial chemicals are most likely to be spilled due to accidents when they are being transported. Liquids like powerful acids will dissolve anything they come into contact with.

SURVIVAL TIPS

Surviving dangerous chemicals

It is unlikely that industrial chemicals will be released by a plant near where you live. If you find out that this has happened, shut all doors and windows immediately.

A more real threat is chemicals in your own home, like cleaning products. These may also be dangerous if they come into contact with skin. If you come in contact with chemicals, wash with lots of water and find fresh air to avoid breathing fumes.

Disasters can happen when we least expect them. More than 50 cars were thrown into the Mississippi River when this bridge collapsed in Minneapolis, Minnesota. Thirteen people died and more than 100 were injured.

BE PREPARED!

Some of the disasters in this book could affect people when they are least prepared. Make sure you are ready for anything by keeping the following items in your home:

Water: Even with no warning of a disaster, most houses will contain some reserves of clean water—for example, in a water tank. If you have warning of a disaster, fill as many containers as possible with clean water. Reserve this water for drinking and cooking. In a disaster, drinking and cooking water should be boiled before use.

Food: Ensure that you have a good store of non-perishable foods, including canned foods. Foods will usually be best stored in a cool, dry area.

Health and hygiene: If essential services fail, health and hygiene are likely to be major issues. You need to have a first-aid kit and cleaning materials.

Heat and light: If power fails, have a plan for how you will cook and keep warm.

You can always add other basic items to your survival supplies. What does your stockpile look like?

Survival in space

Space must be the most extreme place of all to try to survive. That was the challenge for James Lovell, Fred Haise, and John Swigert. These men were part of a space mission that faced disaster in 1970—the Apollo 13 mission to the Moon.

Apollo 13 was planned to be the third mission to land people on the Moon.

The launch went smoothly. Two days into the flight, Lovell and Haise started checking systems on the lunar module, *Aquarius*. This was the part of the ship that would detach from the command module, *Odyssey*, and land them on the Moon.

"Houston, we've had a problem here"

Suddenly, they heard a loud bang. The electrical power failed on *Odyssey*. Swigert contacted mission control in Texas with the words, "Houston, we've had a problem here." It was some time before they

"We came to the slow conclusion that our normal supply of electricity, light, and water was lost, and we were about 200,000 miles from Earth." —James Lovell, astronaut

SURVIVAL SCIENCE

The body in space

Astronauts have to take everything they need to sustain life in space. Space is a vacuum, containing no air or water. In fact, a vacuum contains nothing at all. Astronauts can leave their spacecraft to perform space walks, but without a pressurized spacesuit they would lose consciousness in a few seconds.

U.S. astronaut Garrett Reisman is seen here stranded in space because of an accidental power outage. Luckily this situation did not become a disaster. Power was restored after about half an hour.

realized how big a problem they had. The bang was an **oxygen** tank exploding. It had disabled the equipment that powered the command module. Lovell and Haise would not be landing on the Moon as had been planned. It would be tough enough just to survive.

The three astronauts used *Aquarius* as a lifeboat, since it had enough air, water, and electricity to keep them alive. But they would eventually need *Odyssey*, as it was the only part of the ship that could withstand the intense heat of re-entry into the layer of gases surrounding

Earth. *Aquarius* was not designed to support three astronauts for an extended time. An air purification system designed to absorb carbon dioxide gas as it was breathed out began to fail. Engineers at mission control had to give the astronauts detailed instructions to fit a new one.

Finally, the astronauts moved back to the command module and discarded the *Aquarius* lunar module that had kept them alive. They landed safely in the Pacific Ocean, around 87 hours after the oxygen-tank explosion.

HOW WOULD YOU SURVIVE?

You have read some amazing stories of survival in the face of disaster, ranging from those who survived beneath the rubble of an earthquake to those who survived on their own for weeks on end. In most cases, these people had not been trained to survive. They simply found themselves in the toughest of situations. All of these survivors share some common qualities, which can give us an idea about what it takes to survive.

Endurance

From those who survived in the ruins of the Haiti earthquake to Sergeant John McLoughlin in the ruins of the World Trade Center, the people in this book share the **endurance** and strength to survive until rescue. Often they were in constant pain or desperately trying to find water, but their will to live never weakened.

Adaptability and quick thinking

However prepared you are, disasters are rarely easy to predict. When disaster strikes, survivors need to adapt quickly to the situation. They need to figure out what is important and use what they have around them to survive.

Courage

Those who are caught in natural or human disasters are rarely there by choice. Some, like the rescue service workers who help tackle many disasters, are highly trained to remain calm and do their jobs. Others have to find that courage when things get tough.

Luck

Although the survivors in this book showed extraordinary qualities, luck also played a role in many of their stories. In all the disasters in this book, there were people who shared many of the same qualities, but did not survive because they were in the wrong place at the wrong time. Luck is important, but without the other qualities, luck will only get you so far.

Do you have what it takes?

Can you think of other qualities that helped these people to survive? Do you think you have what it takes to survive when the circumstances look impossible?

Fortunately, most of us will never have to face the same life or death situations that are described in this book. However, we will all need some of these qualities at one time or other. And we all hope that if we found ourselves in a survival situation, we would show the same survival instincts as the people in this book.

Before setting out on a camping or hiking trip, make sure you have all the equipment you need. You may not experience volcanoes, **tornadoes**, or **tsunamis**, but you should always expect the unexpected.

SURVIVAL ESSENTIALS

STORING FOOD

If you are making up a food store or packing food for a journey, choose food that will keep for a long time, such as:

- ✔ wheat, oats, and rice
- ✔ milk and egg powder
- ✔ canned food
- ✔ dried fruit and nuts

Items that will only keep for a limited time include meat, fish, fresh fruits and vegetables, and foods with high fat content. For other foods, check the packaging to see how long it is recommended to keep.

Food should be stored in a cool, dark place. It is also important to keep it dry.

NATURAL SOURCES OF WATER

Water is the most essential item for survival. The easiest source of drinkable water is to capture rain or dew. Rain or dew can be caught in any waterproof container or fabric. There are many natural sources of water:

- ✔ **Desert plants and cacti:** Many desert plants store water in their stems and roots. *WARNING: Not all cacti are safe to drink. The saguaro cactus of North America is poisonous, for example.*
- ✔ **Vines:** Cut a vine as high up as possible with a knife to release water.

- ✔ **Trees:** If you cut banana and plantain trees just above the ground and hollow out the trunk, water will fill the hollow from the roots where it is stored. Some palm trees also contain a sugary fluid that is drinkable.

- ✔ **Animals:** Animal eyes contain water. Fish also contain fluid. Beware of drinking animal fluids, however, as these contain protein and will require more water to digest.

- ✔ **Melting ice and snow:** Melt snow by suspending it in a cloth near a fire, so that it drips into a container. A large amount of snow will only produce a fairly small amount of water. Melting ice will produce more water.

BASIC FIRST-AID KIT

Having a good knowledge of basic first aid can be very important in a survival situation. Always keep a basic first-aid kit in your home and when traveling in remote areas. Try to have the following:

- ✔ plasters or dressings in a range of sizes to protect small cuts and blisters

- ✔ bandages for keeping dressings in place, covering wounds, and keeping broken limbs in place (a large triangular bandage can be used as a sling)

- ✔ scissors and safety pins for cutting and securing bandages

- ✔ **antiseptic** cream and wipes

- ✔ gauze padding to soak up blood and keep wounds clean

- ✔ painkillers

If you or your companions have any specific medical needs, such an allergy to bee stings, make sure you have the proper medicines and equipment in your first-aid kit.

GLOSSARY

aftershock smaller tremors that can happen for several days after a major earthquake

antiseptic substance that prevents the growth of the microorganisms that cause disease

buoy floating marker in the sea used to guide ships

catastrophic disastrous, with terrible effects

contaminate make dirty or polluted. Water that is contaminated will cause disease.

crust outer layer of Earth, made of solid rock

debris wreckage or remains of something that has been destroyed

dehydration when the body suffers from lack of water. This happens when the body uses more water than it takes in.

endurance ability to deal with challenges and keep going

evacuate leave or ask people to leave a place of danger until the danger has passed

hazardous dangerous

hijack take control of something, like an airplane, with force

hurricane tropical storm with very strong, swirling winds. In Asia, a hurricane is called a typhoon or cyclone.

hypothermia condition in which the body loses heat from its core. If untreated, large drops in body temperature can cause death.

lava molten (melted) rock that flows from a volcano

levee protective bank built along a river or coast to prevent flooding

microorganism living thing that can only be seen with a microscope. Bacteria and viruses are microorganisms.

oxygen gas that occurs in Earth's atmosphere and water. Nearly all living things need oxygen to breathe.

plasma fluid part of the blood that is essential for blood to circulate properly

pyroclastic flow super-heated cloud of gas from a volcano

radiation particles (tiny bits) that are given off by radioactive materials, such as uranium, which is used to generate nuclear power

storm surge rise in sea level caused by a storm such as a hurricane

terrorist anyone who seeks to achieve political goals by carrying out acts of violence on people

tornado violent storm made of a swirling funnel of wind that affects a small area

tremor vibration in the earth

tropical happening in the tropics, which is the area of Earth on either side of the equator

tsunami huge wave caused by an undersea earthquake

volcanologist person who studies volcanoes

FIND OUT MORE

BOOKS

Dowswell, Paul. *True Survival Stories*. Eynsham, Witney Oxon, UK: Usborne Books, 2008.

Kalman, Bobbie, and Kelley MacAulay. *Preparing for Disasters (Disaster Alert! series)*. New York, NY: Crabtree, 2009.

Langley, Andrew. *Hurricanes, Tsunamis, and Other Natural Disasters*. Boston, MA: Kingfisher, 2006.

Lewis, Simon. *Survival at Sea (Difficult and Dangerous series)*. Mankato, MN: Smart Apple Media, 2009.

Sandler, Martin W. *America's Great Disasters*. New York, NY: HarperCollins, 2003.

Spilsbury, Louise, and Richard Spilsbury. *Awesome Forces of Nature series*. Chicago, IL: Heinemann Library, 2004.

Vogt, Gregory. *Disasters in Space Exploration*. Minneapolis, MN: Millbrook Press, 2001.

Wheeler, Jill C. *September 11, 2001: The Day that Changed America (War on Terrorism series)*. Edina, MN: ABDO, 2002.

WEBSITES

News websites will give details of specific disasters. When searching for information on the Internet, always be sure that the website you are using is reliable. Is the information provided by an established or official organization? Or, does the site seem to present a biased (one-sided) view? Here are some other websites to try:

www.redcross.org
This is the website of the Red Cross, an organization that helps people when disaster strikes.

www.tsunami.noaa.gov
This National Oceanic and Atmospheric Administration (NOAA) tsunami website has more information about tsunamis and how to be prepared.

www.nhc.noaa.gov
This NOAA website provides up-to-the-minute information about hurricanes.

INDEX